Heart-Healthy Fish

Cooking Light & Healthy with Low-Cholesterol Fish Dishes

by Olivia Rana

Olivia Rana © 2023

License Notes

No part of this Book, either for personal use, commercial use, should be reproduced or distributed without full written permission from the author. This is prohibited by the law.

Also, this book is strictly meant to entertain you. As such, the reader is liable for any damages that the book or its content causes.

Table of Contents

Introduction 6

Additional Useful & Interesting Information 8

  1. Breaded Red Snapper 9

  2. Fish with Tomato & Walnut 11

  3. Halibut with Blueberry Salsa 14

  4. Oat & Walnut Crusted Salmon 17

  5. Tilapia with Parmesan Cheese & Red Pepper 19

  6. Chimichurri Fish 21

  7. Salmon with Dill Sauce 23

  8. Plum Salmon 25

  9. Grilled Mahi Mahi 28

  10. Tilapia with Lemon Sauce 31

  11. Salmon Soup 34

  12. Grilled Tilapia with Mango 37

  13. Halibut Tacos 39

  14. Salmon with Blackberry Sauce 42

  15. Mediterranean Fish 44

  16. Tilapia in Wine Sauce 47

  17. Tuna & White Bean Salad 49

  18. Halibut with Mango 51

19. Roasted Salmon with Spinach 54

20. Tuna Casserole 57

21. Salmon Stir-Fry 60

22. Asian Salmon 63

23. Spiced Salmon 66

24. Spicy Salmon Patties 68

25. Curry Salmon 70

26. Salmon with Lemon & Basil 73

27. Roasted Salmon 75

28. Tuna Casserole with Pimientos 77

29. Salmon & Green Beans 79

30. Tuna Teriyaki Kebab 81

31. Poached Salmon 84

32. Grilled Salmon with Blackberry & Chili Sauce 87

33. Salmon & Potato Salad 89

34. Salmon with Ginger Soy Sauce 92

35. Salmon with White Beans & Spinach 95

36. Salmon with Hoisin & Pineapple Sauce 98

37. Salmon with Brown Sugar Glaze 100

38. Salmon with Orange & Pomegranate 102

39. Mustard Salmon 104

40. Lemon & Basil Salmon 106

41. Ginger Mahi Mahi 108

42. Ginger Honey Salmon 111

43. Tuna Salad 113

44. Tuna Steak & Pasta 115

45. Salmon with Walnuts & Ginger 118

46. Mahi Mahi & Veggies 120

47. Thai Salmon Rice Bowl 122

48. Sage & Garlic Spiced Salmon 124

49. Salmon with Lime & Cucumber Sauce 126

50. Salmon with Horseradish 129

Conclusion 131

Biography 132

Afterword 133

Introduction

If you'd like to turn over a healthier leaf, it'd definitely be a great idea to start including more fish dishes in your diet.

According to the American Heart Association, eating at least two servings of fish a week can help reduce risk of heart disease.

And it's because fish is rich in unsaturated fats known as omega-3 fatty acids.

Omega-3 fatty acids benefit the heart by:

- Reducing triglycerides

- Maintaining proper levels of blood pressure
- Minimizing blood clotting
- Reducing risk of stroke
- Stabilizing heart rhythm

Most types of fish contain omega-3 fatty acids, but most beneficial are fatty fish, which contain more of these. Some of the best options include:

- Salmon
- Cod
- Tuna
- Trout
- Herring

Adults are recommended to consume at least 4-ounce of fish twice a week.

To maximize the health benefits that you can get from eating fish, it's better to prepare it through baking, grilling and broiling. Deep-frying gives you that irresistible crunchy texture but also loads up the fish with fat and calories.

With the recipes that you'll find in this book, you can see how easy and worthwhile it is to cook heart-healthy fish dishes. Even if you're busy with work and other things, you won't have a hard time preparing these recipes.

You'll be doing your heart a huge favor including more of these recipes in your weekly menu!

Don't wait any longer, get started with your healthy diet right away!

Additional Useful & Interesting Information

Omega-3 fatty acids are not only good for the heart but also for one's overall health. Here are the other health benefits that you can get from eating fish:

- Fish supplies you with essential vitamins and minerals such as protein, vitamin D, iron, zinc, potassium, magnesium and iodine.
- Fish can help reduce the risk of stroke and heart disease.
- Fish boosts brain health and wards off neurodegenerative ailments like Alzheimer's Disease.
- Fish decrease the risk of many serious ailments, including diabetes, depression and arthritis.
- Fish can also reduce the risk of asthma by toning down chronic inflammation.

As you can see, fish can benefit your health in many ways, and it's definitely a wise move to include more fish in your regular diet.

1. Breaded Red Snapper

Enjoy every bite into this crunchy and delectable red snapper that's ready in 30 minutes or less. Serve with steamed vegetables on the side.

Serving Size: 4

Preparation & Cooking Time: 30 minutes

Ingredients:

- 2 tablespoons Parmesan cheese, grated
- ½ cup breadcrumbs
- 1 teaspoon lemon pepper seasoning
- Salt to taste
- 24 oz. red snapper fillet, sliced
- 2 tablespoons olive oil

Instructions:

Mix the Parmesan cheese, breadcrumbs, lemon pepper seasoning and salt in a bowl.

Coat the fish fillets with the mixture.

Pour the olive oil into a pan over medium heat.

Cook the fish for 4 to 5 minutes per side or until flaky.

2. Fish with Tomato & Walnut

For sure, you'll reel in compliments with this moist and flavorful fish recipe topped with tomatoes and walnuts. It's simple, but delicious and healthy.

Serving Size: 4

Preparation & Cooking Time: 20 minutes

Ingredients:

- 4 tilapia or any white fish fillets
- Salt and pepper to taste
- Cooking spray
- 1 tablespoon butter
- 1 tomato, sliced thinly

Topping

- ¼ cup walnuts, chopped
- ½ cup breadcrumbs
- 1 ½ teaspoons butter, melted
- 2 tablespoons lemon juice

Instructions:

Season the fish fillets with the salt and pepper.

Spray your pan with oil.

Place the pan over medium heat.

Add the butter.

Once melted, add the fish and cook for 2 to 3 minutes per side.

Transfer the fish to a baking pan.

Top with the tomato.

In a bowl, mix the walnuts, breadcrumbs, butter and lemon juice.

Add the walnut mixture on top of the tomato.

Broil in the oven for 2 to 3 minutes or until the fish is flaky and the topping slightly browned.

3. Halibut with Blueberry Salsa

Blueberries, onion and cilantro dress up halibut fillets in what will easily become a family favorite recipe.

Serving Size: 6

Preparation & Cooking Time: 30 minutes

Ingredients:

- 2 cups blueberries, divided
- 1 onion, chopped
- 1 jalapeno pepper, chopped
- ¼ cup fresh cilantro, minced
- 1 tablespoon balsamic vinegar
- 2 tablespoons orange juice
- 2 tablespoons olive oil, divided
- Salt and pepper to taste
- 6 halibut fillets

Instructions:

Add 1 cup blueberries to a bowl.

Mash with a fork.

Stir in the onion, jalapeno pepper, cilantro, balsamic vinegar and orange juice.

Pour in 1 teaspoon olive oil.

Add the whole blueberries.

Season with the salt.

Mix well.

Cover and refrigerate until ready to serve.

Coat the halibut fillets with the remaining oil.

Season with the salt and pepper.

Grill the fish over medium heat for 3 to 5 minutes per side or until flaky.

Top with the salsa before serving.

4. Oat & Walnut Crusted Salmon

Give salmon a new spin with this incredible recipe that you can prepare in just a few minutes. It looks elegant and fancy but it's actually effortless. Opt for wild-caught salmon if available.

Serving Size: 2

Preparation & Cooking Time: 30 minutes

Ingredients:

- 2 salmon fillets, skin removed
- Salt and pepper to taste
- 2 tablespoons olive oil
- 3 tablespoons walnuts, chopped
- 3 tablespoons oats (quick-cooking)

Instructions:

Preheat your oven to 400 degrees F.

Add the salmon to a baking pan.

Season with the salt and pepper.

In a bowl, mix the olive oil, walnuts and oats.

Press the mixture onto the walnuts.

Bake the fish in the oven for 13 to 15 minutes or until flaky.

5. Tilapia with Parmesan Cheese & Red Pepper

You'll enjoy the savory, cheesy and spicy flavors of this tilapia dish. And it's baked, not fried so it's a healthy option that would be a good addition to your weekly menu.

Serving Size: 4

Preparation & Cooking Time: 20 minutes

Ingredients:

- 1 egg, beaten
- 1 teaspoon Italian seasoning
- 1 teaspoon red pepper flakes, crushed
- ½ cup Parmesan cheese, grated
- Pepper to taste
- 4 tilapia fillets

Instructions:

Preheat your oven to 425 degrees F.

Add the egg to a bowl.

In another bowl, mix the Italian seasoning, red pepper flakes, Parmesan cheese and pepper.

Dip the fish in the egg and then coat with the Parmesan cheese mixture.

Transfer the fish in a baking pan.

Bake in the oven for 10 to 15 minutes or until flaky.

6. Chimichurri Fish

Here's a light fish recipe that's packed not only with flavor but also with health benefits. It's a great idea whether for a simple night or when you're having guests over at your home.

Serving Size: 4

Preparation & Cooking Time: 30 minutes

Ingredients:

- 4 white fish fillets
- ¼ teaspoon garlic salt
- ½ cup olive oil
- 4 teaspoons lemon juice
- 2 tablespoons fresh parsley, chopped
- 2 tablespoons fresh thyme, chopped
- 2 tablespoons fresh oregano, chopped
- 2 tablespoons fresh chives, chopped
- 2 tablespoons fresh basil, chopped

Garnish

- Lemon wedges

Instructions:

Preheat your oven to 350 degrees F.

Place the white fish fillets in a baking pan.

Season the fish with the garlic salt.

Bake the fish in the oven for 20 minutes or until flaky.

In a bowl, mix the olive oil, lemon juice, parsley, thyme, oregano, chives and basil.

Pour the herb mixture over the fish fillets.

Garnish with the lemon wedges before serving.

7. Salmon with Dill Sauce

Flavor up salmon with creamy and tasty dill sauce in this dish that's ready in just a few minutes. Serve this dish with roasted potatoes or steamed vegetables on the side.

Serving Size: 4

Preparation & Cooking Time: 30 minutes

Ingredients:

- 1 tablespoon canola oil
- 4 salmon fillets
- Salt to taste
- 1 teaspoon Italian seasoning
- ¼ cup low fat mayonnaise
- ½ cup low fat plain yogurt
- 1 teaspoon fresh dill, snipped
- ¼ cup cucumber, chopped

Instructions:

Pour the canola oil into a pan over medium high heat.

Season the salmon fillets with the salt and Italian seasoning.

Once the oil is hot, add the salmon to the pan.

Reduce the heat to medium.

Cook the fish for 5 minutes per side or until flaky.

In a bowl, mix the mayonnaise, yogurt, dill and cucumber.

Serve the mayo mixture on top of the fish fillet.

8. Plum Salmon

This will easily become a family favorite recipe. It can also be your go-to recipe for busy nights since it's hassle-free to make.

Serving Size: 6

Preparation & Cooking Time: 35 minutes

Ingredients:

- 5 plums, divided
- ½ cup water
- 1 tablespoon olive oil
- 1 chipotle pepper in adobo sauce, chopped
- 2 tablespoons ketchup
- 1 tablespoon sugar
- 6 salmon fillets
- Salt to taste

Instructions:

Dice 2 plums and add to a saucepan over medium heat.

Cover with water.

Bring to a boil.

Reduce heat and simmer for 15 minutes.

Transfer the boiled plums to a food processor.

Add the olive oil, chipotle pepper with adobo sauce, ketchup and sugar.

Process until smooth.

Reserve ¾ cup of the mixture for serving.

Season the salmon with the salt.

Grill over medium heat for 5 minutes per side, brushing with the remaining plum mixture.

Slice the remaining 3 plums.

Serve the salmon with the reserved sauce and garnish with the plum slices.

9. Grilled Mahi Mahi

If you're looking for healthier options, this grilled mahi mahi should make it to your list. Not only is this packed with essential nutrients, you'll also love how the mango salsa complements the grilled fish.

Serving Size: 8

Preparation & Cooking Time: 30 minutes

Ingredients:

- 2 cloves garlic, minced
- 2 tablespoons pineapple juice
- ¾ cup low sodium teriyaki sauce
- 8 mahi mahi fillets

Salsa

- ½ onion, minced
- ¾ cup green pepper, chopped
- 1 mango, peeled and sliced into cubes
- ½ cup pineapple chunks
- 1 cup papaya, peeled, seeded and chopped
- ¼ cup fresh cilantro, minced
- ¼ cup fresh mint, minced
- ½ teaspoon red pepper flakes
- 1 tablespoon jalapeno pepper, chopped
- 1 tablespoon lemon juice
- 1 tablespoon lime juice

Instructions:

In a shallow dish, mix the garlic, pineapple juice and teriyaki sauce.

Add the mahi mahi and turn to coat with the sauce.

Cover and refrigerate for 30 minutes.

In a bowl, mix the onion, green pepper, mango, pineapple chunks, papaya, cilantro, mint and red pepper flakes.

Stir in the lemon juice and lime juice.

Cover the bowl and refrigerate until ready to serve.

Grill the mahi mahi fillets over medium heat for 4 to 5 minutes per side.

Serve with the mango salsa on the side.

10. Tilapia with Lemon Sauce

Instead of the usual main courses that you serve all the time, why don't you try this amazingly easy tilapia with lemon sauce recipe? For sure, you're going to get rave reviews from everyone!

Serving Size: 4

Preparation & Cooking Time: 30 minutes

Ingredients:

- ¼ cup all purpose flour
- Salt to taste
- 4 tilapia fillets
- 2 tablespoons butter
- 2 teaspoons butter
- 1 tablespoon all-purpose flour
- 1/3 cup low sodium chicken broth
- 1 ½ teaspoons lemon juice
- 2 tablespoons white wine
- 1 ½ teaspoons fresh parsley, minced
- 2 cups hot cooked rice
- ¼ cup almonds, toasted and sliced

Instructions:

Add ¼ cup all purpose flour and salt to a bowl.

Coat the fish fillets with the flour mixture.

Add 2 tablespoons butter to a pan over medium high heat.

Cook the fish for 4 to 5 minutes per side.

Transfer the fish to a plate.

Add the remaining butter to the same pan.

Stir in the remaining flour.

Add the broth, lemon juice, white wine and parsley.

Bring to a boil.

Reduce heat and simmer for 2 minutes.

Serve the fish with the sauce and rice.

Garnish with the almonds.

11. Salmon Soup

Prepare this salmon soup to experience comfort during chilly nights. Serve with toasted bread.

Serving Size: 2

Preparation & Cooking Time: 30 minutes

Ingredients:

- 1 ½ cups water
- 1 cup low sodium chicken broth
- 1 carrot, sliced into cubes
- 1 potato, peeled and sliced into cubes
- 5 fresh mushrooms, sliced in half
- 1 tablespoon all purpose flour
- ¼ cup low fat evaporated milk
- ¼ cup mozzarella cheese, shredded
- ½ lb. salmon fillet, sliced
- Salt and pepper to taste
- 1 tablespoon fresh dill, chopped

Instructions:

Pour the water and chicken broth into a pot over medium heat.

Stir in the carrot and potato.

Bring to a boil.

Reduce heat to medium.

Cook for 15 minutes or until vegetables are tender.

Add the mushrooms.

In a bowl, mix the all purpose flour and evaporated milk.

Add this to the soup.

Return to a boil.

Reduce heat to medium.

Cook while stirring until the cheese has melted.

Add the salmon.

Cook until the fish is flaky.

Season with the salt and pepper.

Sprinkle with the fresh dill before serving.

12. Grilled Tilapia with Mango

This is a special treat that's easy enough to cook on busy nights!

Serving Size: 4

Preparation & Cooking Time: 20 minutes

Ingredients:

- 4 tilapia fillets
- 1 tablespoon olive oil
- ½ teaspoon dill weed
- Salt and pepper to taste
- 1 lemon, sliced
- 1 mango, peeled and sliced thinly
- 1 tablespoon Parmesan cheese, grated

Instructions:

Brush both sides of the tilapia fillets with the olive oil.

Season with the dill weed, salt and pepper.

Grill the fish over medium heat for 5 minutes per side.

Top with the lemon and mango.

Sprinkle with Parmesan cheese.

Grill for 2 to 3 minutes more.

13. Halibut Tacos

Here's a delectable twist to the usual tacos that you serve at home. You'll all enjoy the combination of fish, mango, avocado, onion and sweet chili sauce. If you want it even healthier, you can swap tortillas with lettuce leaves.

Serving Size: 4

Preparation & Cooking Time: 30 minutes

Ingredients:

- ¼ cup red onion, chopped
- 2 tablespoons jalapeno pepper, seeded and chopped
- ½ cup avocado, peeled, pitted and sliced into cubes
- 1 mango, peeled and cubed
- 1 tablespoon fresh cilantro, minced
- 3 teaspoons olive oil, divided
- 1 teaspoon honey
- 1 teaspoon lemon juice
- 1 lb. halibut steaks
- Salt and pepper to taste
- 4 lettuce leaves, chopped
- 4 flour tortillas, warmed
- 4 teaspoons sweet Thai chili sauce

Instructions:

Combine the red onion, jalapeno pepper, avocado, mango and cilantro.

Stir in 1 teaspoon olive oil, honey and lemon juice.

Mix well and set aside.

Brush both sides of the halibut with the remaining olive oil.

Season with the salt and pepper.

Grill the halibut over medium high heat for 3 to 5 minutes per side.

Transfer to a cutting board and slice into cubes.

Top the tortillas with the chopped lettuce, mango mixture and cubed fish.

Drizzle with the sweet chili sauce.

14. Salmon with Blackberry Sauce

Get endless compliments each time you serve this dish—grilled salmon with sweet savory blackberry sauce.

Serving Size: 6

Preparation & Cooking Time: 40 minutes

Ingredients:

- 2 cups fresh blackberries
- 1 ½ teaspoons honey
- 1 ½ teaspoons chipotle hot pepper sauce
- 1 tablespoon brown sugar
- 2 tablespoons white wine
- Salt and pepper to taste
- 1 clove garlic, minced
- ¼ cup shallots, chopped
- 6 salmon fillets

Instructions:

Add the blackberries, honey, chipotle hot pepper sauce, brown sugar, white wine, salt and pepper to a food processor.

Process until pureed.

Strain the mixture and discard the seeds.

Add the garlic and shallots.

Season the salmon with the salt and pepper.

Grill over medium heat for 3 to 5 minutes or until flaky.

Serve the grilled fish with the blackberry sauce.

15. Mediterranean Fish

Here's a delicious fish dish that will become your go-to recipe whenever you're craving for something rich and tasty. This recipe works well for any white fish fillet.

Serving Size: 4

Preparation & Cooking Time: 30 minutes

Ingredients:

- 1 lb. white fish fillets, sliced
- Pepper to taste
- 1 lemon, sliced
- 2 tablespoons white wine
- 2 tablespoons olive oil, divided
- 2 cloves garlic, minced
- 2 cups cherry tomatoes, sliced in half
- ½ cup Greek olives, sliced in half
- 1 tablespoon lemon juice
- 1 tablespoon capers, drained
- 2 tablespoons fresh parsley, minced

Instructions:

Preheat your oven to 400 degrees F.

Season the fish fillets with the pepper.

Place on top of a foil sheet.

Top with the lemon slices, and drizzle with the white wine and half of the olive oil.

In a bowl, mix the remaining olive oil, garlic, cherry tomatoes, Greek olives, lemon juice and capers.

Fold the foil around the fish and seal tightly.

Place the foil packets on a baking pan.

Bake in the oven for 10 to 15 minutes.

Open the foil sheet.

Sprinkle with the fresh parsley before serving.

16. Tilapia in Wine Sauce

Steaming is one of the healthiest ways to cook fish. But don't make the mistake of thinking that this results in a bland dish. Here's a steamed tilapia recipe that tantalizes your taste buds.

Serving Size: 4

Preparation & Cooking Time: 20 minutes

Ingredients:

- 4 tilapia fillets
- Salt and pepper to taste
- 4 tablespoons butter
- 2 tablespoons chives, minced
- 1 lb. sugar snap peas, trimmed
- ½ cup white wine
- Cooked rice

Instructions:

Season the fish fillets with salt and pepper.

Place the fish fillets on top of a foil sheet.

Top the fish fillets with the butter, chives and sugar snap peas.

Drizzle with the wine.

Fold the foil and seal the edges.

Grill the foil packet over medium heat for 15 minutes.

Open the foil sheet carefully.

Serve with the rice.

17. Tuna & White Bean Salad

Don't be surprised if this becomes a regular request at your house. Fast and easy to put together, this salad should definitely become part of your meal routine.

Serving Size: 4

Preparation & Cooking Time: 15 minutes

Ingredients:

- 4 cups fresh arugula
- 15 oz. cannellini beans, rinsed and drained
- 1 cup grape tomatoes, sliced in half
- ½ red onion, sliced thinly
- 1/3 cup roasted sweet red peppers, chopped
- 1/3 cup olives, pitted
- ¼ cup fresh basil, chopped
- 3 tablespoons olive oil
- 2 tablespoons lemon juice
- ½ teaspoon lemon zest
- 1 clove garlic, minced
- Salt to taste
- 10 oz. white tuna flakes in water

Instructions:

Combine the arugula, cannellini beans, tomatoes, sweet peppers, olives and basil in a bowl.

Mix the olive oil, lemon juice, lemon zest, garlic and salt.

Pour the dressing over the salad.

Stir in the tuna.

Toss gently and serve.

18. Halibut with Mango

This is a quick, healthy and delicious fish recipe that's special enough to make for guests--halibut marinated first in spices before simmered in savory coconut milk sauce and served on top of spinach.

Serving Size: 6

Preparation & Cooking Time: 50 minutes

Ingredients:

- 2 teaspoons curry powder
- 2 teaspoons ground coriander
- ½ teaspoon ground allspice
- 1 teaspoon chili powder
- Salt and pepper to taste
- 2 lb. halibut fillets, sliced into cubes
- 5 tablespoons canola oil, divided
- 1 onion, sliced into wedges
- 2 sweet red peppers, sliced
- 13 oz. coconut milk
- 2 mangoes, peeled and sliced into cubes
- 3 tablespoons tomato paste
- 10 oz. spinach, torn

Instructions:

Mix the curry powder, ground coriander, ground allspice and chili powder in a bowl.

Sprinkle the halibut with the mixture.

Cover and refrigerate for 30 minutes.

Add 1 tablespoon canola oil to a pan over medium heat.

Sauté the onion and sweet red peppers for 4 to 5 minutes or until tender.

Transfer to a plate and set aside.

Add 2 tablespoons canola oil to the same pan.

Cook the halibut for 3 to 4 minutes per side.

Pour in the coconut milk.

Stir in the mango and tomato paste.

Add the sweet pepper mixture.

Cook for 5 minutes.

In another pan, cook the spinach in the remaining oil until wilted.

Serve the fish on top of the spinach.

19. Roasted Salmon with Spinach

This instantly transforms a regular night into something delightful—roasted salmon served on a bed of spinach and tomatoes.

Serving Size: 4

Preparation & Cooking Time: 30 minutes

Ingredients:

- 3 teaspoons olive oil, divided
- 4 salmon fillets
- Pepper to taste
- 1 ½ teaspoons low sodium seafood seasoning
- Pinch red pepper flakes
- 1 clove garlic, sliced
- 10 cups fresh baby spinach
- 6 tomatoes, sliced
- ½ cup balsamic vinegar

Instructions:

Preheat your oven to 450 degrees F.

Drizzle the salmon with 1 teaspoon olive oil.

Season with the pepper and seafood seasoning.

Transfer the fish to a baking pan.

Roast the fish inside the oven for 5 to 10 minutes or until flaky.

In a pot over medium heat, add the remaining oil, pepper flakes and garlic.

Cook for 3 to 4 minutes or until garlic is softened.

Add the spinach.

Cook for 4 to 5 minutes or until wilted.

Add the tomatoes.

Place the spinach mixture on serving plates.

Add the vinegar to a pan over medium heat and bring to a boil.

Cook until reduced to half.

Serve the salmon on top of the spinach mixture.

Drizzle with the vinegar.

20. Tuna Casserole

Affordable, fast and flavorful—this dish won't leave you wanting! And because it costs less than other fish dishes, this won't leave your pockets empty either.

Serving Size: 6

Preparation & Cooking Time: 40 minutes

Ingredients:

- 3 tablespoons butter, divided
- 1 onion, chopped
- 1 cup Portobello mushrooms, sliced
- 1 sweet red pepper, chopped
- 4 carrots, peeled and chopped
- 2 cups baby spinach
- 1 cup peas
- 10 oz. white tuna flakes in water, drained
- 3 cups spiral pasta (uncooked)
- 1 tablespoon all purpose flour
- 1/3 cup half and half cream
- 2/3 cup reduced sodium chicken broth
- ½ cup Parmesan cheese, shredded
- Salt and pepper to taste

Instructions:

Add 1 tablespoon butter to a pan over medium high heat.

Cook the onion, mushrooms, sweet red pepper and carrots for 10 minutes, stirring often.

Stir in the spinach, peas and tuna flakes.

Cook for 2 to 3 minutes or until spinach is wilted.

Cook the pasta according to the directions in the package.

Drain but reserve 1 cup water.

Add the pasta and tuna mixture to a bowl.

Toss gently to combine.

Add the remaining butter to the same pan.

Stir in the flour, cream and broth.

Cook while stirring for 2 minutes, adding the reserved pasta water.

Stir in the Parmesan cheese.

Season with the salt and pepper.

Pour the mixture over the pasta.

Toss to coat, and serve.

21. Salmon Stir-Fry

You'll love how flavorful and easy to make this salmon stir fry is! Using stir-fry vegetable mix definitely saves a lot of time and effort.

Serving Size: 4

Preparation & Cooking Time: 30 minutes

Ingredients:

- 2 tablespoons orange juice
- 1 tablespoon low sodium soy sauce
- ¼ cup low fat honey mustard salad dressing
- 1 tablespoon ginger, minced
- 1 teaspoon orange zest
- 1 tablespoon molasses
- 4 teaspoons canola oil, divided
- 1 lb. salmon fillets, skin removed and sliced into cubes
- 16 oz. frozen stir-fry vegetable mix
- Hot cooked brown rice
- 1 tablespoon white sesame seeds, toasted

Instructions:

Combine the orange juice, soy sauce, honey mustard salad dressing, ginger, orange zest and molasses in a bowl.

Add 2 teaspoons canola oil to a pan over medium heat.

Cook the salmon for 3 to 5 minutes, stirring often.

Transfer to a plate.

Add the remaining oil to the same pan.

Cook the vegetable blend for 2 to 3 minutes.

Pour in the salad dressing mixture.

Return the salmon to the pan.

Heat through for 3 to 5 minutes.

Serve with the rice and sprinkle with the sesame seeds.

22. Asian Salmon

If you love salmon, you'll love it even more when you discover more ways to cook it. Here's another fantastic idea that's surely worth a try—season salmon with chili sauce, garlic and lime juice, and wrap in foil before cooking in the oven. You'll be delighted with the result.

Serving Size: 4

Preparation & Cooking Time: 30 minutes

Ingredients:

- 1 sweet onion, sliced
- 4 salmon fillets
- 1 tablespoon sesame oil
- 1 tablespoon lime juice
- 3 tablespoons chili sauce
- 1 clove garlic, minced
- 1 teaspoon ginger, minced
- 1 teaspoon mustard seed
- ½ teaspoon black sesame seeds
- Lime zest
- Fresh mint leaves, chopped

Instructions:

Preheat your oven to 400 degrees F.

Divide the onion slices among 4 sheets of foil.

Add 1 salmon on top of the onion on each foil sheet.

In a bowl, mix the sesame oil, lime juice, chili sauce, garlic, ginger, mustard seed and black sesame seeds.

Pour the mixture on top of the salmon.

Fold the salmon and pinch the edges to seal.

Place the foil packets in a baking pan.

Bake in the oven for 15 to 20 minutes.

Open the foil packets carefully.

Garnish with the lime zest and mint leaves before serving.

23. Spiced Salmon

Here's another exciting way to prepare salmon—flavor it up with a mix of soy sauce, sugar, butter, herbs and spices before cooking on the grill.

Serving Size: 8

Preparation & Cooking Time: 20 minutes

Ingredients:

- 2 lb. salmon fillet
- 1 tablespoon olive oil
- 1 tablespoon soy sauce
- 2 tablespoons brown sugar
- 1 tablespoon melted butter
- ½ teaspoon ground mustard
- ½ teaspoon garlic powder
- ¼ teaspoon dill weed
- ½ teaspoon pepper
- ¼ teaspoon dried tarragon
- ½ teaspoon paprika
- Pinch cayenne pepper
- Salt to taste

Instructions:

Place the salmon in a baking pan.

In a bowl, mix all the ingredients.

Brush the mixture on both sides of the salmon.

Grill the salmon over medium heat for 10 to 15 minutes or until flaky.

24. Spicy Salmon Patties

These spicy salmon patties are easy to prepare. And you'll love how the flavors come together in each bite. Serve with a fresh green salad and garnish with lemon wedges.

Serving Size: 4

Preparation & Cooking Time: 30 minutes

Ingredients:

- ½ cup onion, chopped
- 2 cloves garlic, minced
- 14 ¾ oz. salmon flakes
- 1/3 cup green pepper, chopped
- 1 tablespoon jalapeno pepper chopped
- ¼ cup breadcrumbs
- 2 teaspoons Italian seasoning
- 2 teaspoons spicy seasoning blend
- 2 eggs, beaten
- Pepper to taste
- 2 tablespoons olive oil

Instructions:

Combine all the ingredients except olive oil in a bowl.

Mix gently.

Add the oil to a pan over medium heat.

Then, cook the patties for 4 to 5 minutes per side or until golden brown.

25. Curry Salmon

Enjoy this curry-flavored salmon dish that's both simple and elegant. Serve with brown rice and steamed beans.

Serving Size: 4

Preparation & Cooking Time: 30 minutes

Ingredients:

- 4 salmon fillets
- 2 tablespoons green curry paste
- 1 cup coconut milk
- 1 cup instant brown rice (uncooked)
- 1 cup low sodium chicken broth
- Pepper to taste
- ¾ lb. green beans, trimmed and steamed
- 1 teaspoon sesame seeds
- Lime wedges

Instructions:

Preheat your oven to 400 degrees F.

Add the salmon to a baking pan.

In a bowl, mix the green curry paste and coconut milk.

Pour the mixture over the salmon.

Bake in the oven for 15 to 20 minutes or until the fish is flaky.

In a pan over medium heat, combine the instant brown rice, chicken broth and pepper.

Bring to a boil.

Reduce heat and simmer for 5 minutes.

Turn off the stove.

Let sit for 5 minutes.

Serve the fish with the brown rice and steamed green beans.

Pour the sauce on top, and garnish with the sesame seeds and lime wedges.

26. Salmon with Lemon & Basil

A refreshing way to prepare and cook salmon—top it with lemon and basil and drizzle with olive oil before baking in the oven. It's light, tasty, and enticing!

Serving Size: 4

Preparation & Cooking Time: 30 minutes

Ingredients:

- 4 salmon fillets
- 2 teaspoons olive oil
- Salt and pepper to taste
- 2 tablespoons fresh basil, sliced thinly
- 1 tablespoon lemon zest
- 2 lemons, sliced thinly

Instructions:

Preheat your oven to 375 degrees F.

Add the salmon to a baking pan.

Drizzle with the olive oil.

Season with the salt and pepper.

Top with the lemon zest, lemon slices and basil.

Bake in the oven for 15 to 20 minutes or until flaky.

27. Roasted Salmon

For an easy and hassle-free dinner, try this roasted salmon recipe. It's a good option if you'd like something tasty but healthy for dinner. Use center-cut salmon for this recipe.

Serving Size: 4

Preparation & Cooking Time: 20 minutes

Ingredients:

- 1 ½ lb. salmon fillet
- 1 tablespoon olive oil
- Salt and pepper to taste

Instructions:

Place a cast-iron skillet inside your oven.

Preheat your oven to 450 degrees F.

Brush both sides of the salmon with the olive oil.

Season with the salt and pepper.

Place the fish in the skillet.

Bake the fish for 15 to 17 minutes or until the internal temperature reaches 125 degrees F.

Slice the salmon into 4 portions and serve.

28. Tuna Casserole with Pimientos

When you want a fast but satisfying meal after a tiring day at work, this is the ideal recipe to prepare—tuna casserole with pimiento, cheese and crushed cornflakes. It comes out from the oven beautifully in less than 1 hour.

Serving Size: 5

Preparation & Cooking Time: 40 minutes

Ingredients:

- 7 oz. elbow macaroni
- 10 ¾ oz. cream of mushroom soup
- 1 cup nonfat milk
- 1 cup cheddar cheese, shredded
- 1 cup mushrooms, sliced
- 2 tablespoons pimientos, diced
- 3 teaspoons dried onion, minced
- 5 oz. tuna flakes in water, drained
- 1 teaspoon ground mustard
- Salt to taste
- 1/3 cup cornflakes, crushed

Instructions:

Cook the elbow macaroni according to the directions in the package.

Drain and transfer to a bowl.

In another bowl, mix the cream of mushroom soup, nonfat milk, cheddar cheese, mushrooms, pimientos, dried onion, tuna flakes, ground mustard and salt.

Stir in the macaroni.

Transfer the mixture to a baking pan.

Top with the crushed cornflakes.

Bake in the oven at 350 degrees F for 30 minutes.

29. Salmon & Green Beans

Satisfy your cravings for comfort food with this salmon and green beans recipe without the hassle and without the extra calories or fat. If you'd like to infuse it with Asian flavors, swap olive oil with sesame oil and flavor up the fish with minced ginger.

Serving Size: 4

Preparation & Cooking Time: 35 minutes

Ingredients:

- 4 salmon fillets
- Cooking spray
- 1 tablespoon olive oil
- 1 tablespoon butter
- 2 tablespoons low sodium soy sauce
- 2 tablespoons brown sugar
- 2 tablespoons Dijon mustard
- Salt and pepper to taste
- 1 lb. green beans, trimmed

Instructions:

Preheat your oven to 425 degrees F.

Arrange the fish fillets in a baking pan sprayed with oil.

Add the butter to a pan over medium heat.

Stir in the olive oil, butter, soy sauce, brown sugar, Dijon mustard, salt and pepper.

Brush both sides of the salmon with half of the mixture.

Add the green beans to the remaining mixture.

Place the green beans around the salmon.

Roast in the oven for 15 minutes or until fish is flaky.

30. Tuna Teriyaki Kebab

If you're looking for a new way to cook tuna, here's a recipe that you must definitely try—tuna kebabs flavored with sweet savory teriyaki sauce.

Serving Size: 8

Preparation & Cooking Time: 40 minutes

Ingredients:

- 1 ½ lb. tuna steaks, sliced into cubes
- 1 sweet onion, sliced
- 2 sweet red peppers, sliced

Marinade / Sauce

- ¼ cup sesame oil
- 2 tablespoons olive oil
- 2 tablespoons soy sauce
- 3 tablespoons lime juice
- ¼ cup fresh cilantro, minced
- 2 cloves garlic, minced
- 1 tablespoon ginger, minced

Salad

- 5 oz. baby spinach
- 8 cherry tomatoes, sliced in half
- 1 sweet yellow pepper, sliced

Instructions:

Thread the tuna steaks onto skewers.

Thread the sweet onion and sweet red peppers onto other skewers.

Place the skewers in a baking pan.

In a bowl, mix the sesame oil, olive oil, soy sauce, lime juice, cilantro, garlic and ginger.

Divide the marinade into 2 portions.

Add the first portion to the baking pan and marinate the kebabs in the refrigerator for 30 minutes.

Grill the fish kebabs for 3 to 5 minutes per side, and the vegetable kebabs for 5 to 6 minutes per side.

Toss together the spinach, cherry tomatoes and yellow pepper in a bowl.

Stir in the reserved mixture.

Serve the kebabs with the salad.

31. Poached Salmon

Don't want anything heavy for dinner? Here's the perfect option. You'll even have room for dessert!

Serving Size: 4

Preparation & Cooking Time: 1 hour and 40 minutes

Ingredients:

- 2 cups water
- 2 tablespoons lemon juice
- 1 cup white wine
- 1 onion, sliced
- 1 carrot, sliced
- 1 rib celery, sliced
- 1 sprig fresh rosemary
- 3 sprigs fresh thyme
- 1 bay leaf
- Salt and pepper to taste
- 4 salmon fillets
- 1 cup water
- Lemon wedges

Instructions:

Pour the water, lemon juice and white wine into a slow cooker.

Stir in the onion, celery, carrot, herbs, bay leaf, salt and pepper.

Cover the pot.

Cook on low 45 minutes.

Add the salmon fillets to the pot.

Pour in the water.

Cook for 45 minutes or until flaky.

Drain the liquid.

Serve the fish garnished with the lemon wedges.

32. Grilled Salmon with Blackberry & Chili Sauce

You'll love how healthy and effortless this salmon dish is! It's a no-fail recipe that impresses everyone each time.

Serving Size: 4

Preparation & Cooking Time: 30 minutes

Ingredients:

- 2 tablespoons sweet chili sauce, divided
- 1 cup blackberries
- 1 green onion, minced
- 1 cup zucchini, chopped
- 4 salmon fillets
- Salt and pepper to taste

Instructions:

Combine 1 tablespoon sweet chili sauce with blackberries, green onion and zucchini in a bowl.

Mix well.

Season the salmon with salt and pepper.

Grill the salmon over medium high heat for 5 to 6 minutes per side, brushing with the remaining chili sauce.

Top the grilled salmon with the blackberry sauce.

33. Salmon & Potato Salad

Let this recipe be your inspiration for your next culinary masterpiece! But actually, it's very easy to make, and will only take you 30 minutes to prepare.

Serving Size: 4

Preparation & Cooking Time: 30 minutes

Ingredients:

- 1 lb. fingerling potatoes, sliced in half
- ½ lb. fresh asparagus, trimmed and sliced
- ½ lb. fresh green beans, trimmed and sliced
- Water
- 4 salmon fillets
- 1 tablespoon red wine vinaigrette
- Salt and pepper to taste
- 1/3 cup red wine vinaigrette
- 1 tablespoon fresh chives, minced
- 4 cups baby spinach
- 2 cups cherry tomatoes, sliced in half

Instructions:

Add the potatoes to a pot.

Cover with water.

Bring to a boil.

Reduce heat and simmer for 15 minutes.

Add the asparagus and green beans in the last 4 minutes of cooking.

Drain and set aside.

Brush both sides of the salmon with 1 tablespoon red wine vinaigrette.

Season the salmon with salt and pepper.

Grill the salmon over medium high heat for 3 to 4 minutes per side or until flaky.

Mix the potato mixture, chives, spinach and tomatoes.

Drizzle with the vinaigrette.

Top with the salmon and serve.

34. Salmon with Ginger Soy Sauce

If you'd like a healthier lifestyle, this recipe should make it to your list. This salmon dish flavored with sweet savory ginger soy sauce is surely satisfying.

Serving Size: 4

Preparation & Cooking Time: 30 minutes

Ingredients:

- 1 tablespoon cornstarch
- 2 tablespoons all purpose flour
- 4 salmon fillets
- 1 tablespoon canola oil
- 1/3 cup apple juice
- 2 green onions, minced
- ½ teaspoon garlic powder
- ¼ cup ginger, minced
- 3 tablespoons soy sauce
- 1 tablespoon balsamic vinegar
- 2 tablespoons honey

Instructions:

Mix the cornstarch and all purpose flour.

Coat the salmon fillets with the cornstarch mixture.

Pour the canola oil into a pan over medium high heat for 5 minutes per side or until flaky.

Transfer to a plate.

Tent with a foil to keep warm.

Pour in the apple juice.

Scrape the browned bits with a wooden spoon.

Stir in the green onions, garlic powder, ginger, soy sauce, balsamic vinegar and honey.

Cook while stirring for 2 minutes.

Serve the salmon with the sauce.

35. Salmon with White Beans & Spinach

Serve with spinach and white beans, this salmon dish easily becomes a favorite meal even on busy nights.

Serving Size: 4

Preparation & Cooking Time: 15 minutes

Ingredients:

- 4 salmon fillets
- 2 teaspoons olive oil
- 1 teaspoon seafood seasoning
- 1 tablespoon olive oil
- 1 clove garlic, minced
- 15 oz. white beans, rinsed and drained
- Salt and pepper to taste
- 8 oz. spinach
- Lemon wedges

Instructions:

Preheat your broiler.

Brush the salmon fillets with 2 teaspoons olive oil.

Sprinkle with the seafood seasoning.

Place the salmon in a broiler pan.

Broil in the oven for 6 to 7 minutes or until flaky.

Pour the remaining oil into a pan over medium heat.

Cook the garlic for 30 seconds, stirring often.

Add the white beans.

Season with the salt and pepper.

Stir in the spinach.

Cook until wilted.

Transfer to a serving plate.

Top with the salmon and garnish with the lemon wedges.

36. Salmon with Hoisin & Pineapple Sauce

This salmon drenched with pineapple and hoisin sauce will win you over and over again. You'll fall in love at first bite.

Serving Size: 4

Preparation & Cooking Time: 20 minutes

Ingredients:

- 4 salmon fillets
- 2 tablespoons hoisin sauce
- Pepper to taste
- ¼ cup orange marmalade
- ½ cup pineapple chunks
- 2 tablespoons fresh cilantro, chopped

Instructions:

Preheat your oven to 400 degrees F.

Brush the salmon with the hoisin sauce.

Season with the pepper.

Place the salmon in a baking pan.

Bake in the oven for 15 minutes or until flaky.

Add the orange marmalade to a pan over medium heat.

Stir in the pineapple chunks.

Cook while stirring for 5 minutes.

Spoon the sauce over the salmon.

Top with the cilantro and serve.

37. Salmon with Brown Sugar Glaze

Your mouth will water each time you think of a salmon fillet beautifully covered with sweet glaze. It's a delightful treat you can enjoy for lunch or dinner.

Serving Size: 8

Preparation & Cooking Time: 35 minutes

Ingredients:

- 2 teaspoons butter
- 1 tablespoon brown sugar
- 1 teaspoon honey
- 1 tablespoon olive oil
- 1 tablespoon soy sauce
- 1 tablespoon Dijon mustard
- Salt and pepper to taste
- 2 ½ lb. salmon fillet

Instructions:

Add the butter, brown sugar and honey to a pan over medium heat.

Cook while stirring until melted.

Turn off heat.

Stir in the olive oil, soy sauce, Dijon mustard, salt and pepper.

Let cool for 5 minutes.

Place the salmon in a baking pan.

Spread the sugar mixture on top.

Bake in the oven at 350 degrees F for 25 to 30 minutes or until flaky.

38. Salmon with Orange & Pomegranate

Even if you're not a salmon lover, you'll have a change of heart once you give this amazingly easy recipe a try.

Serving Size: 4

Preparation & Cooking Time: 35 minutes

Ingredients:

- 1 red onion, sliced thinly
- 2 lb. salmon fillet, skin removed
- Salt to taste
- 1 orange, sliced thinly
- 1 cup pomegranate seeds
- 2 tablespoons olive oil
- 1 tablespoon fresh dill, minced

Instructions:

Preheat your oven to 375 degrees F.

Spread the onion slices in a baking pan.

Top with the salmon fillet.

Season with the salt.

Place the orange slices on top and sprinkle with the pomegranate seeds.

Drizzle with the olive oil.

Cover the pan with foil.

Bake the fish in the oven for 30 minutes.

Sprinkle with the dill before serving.

39. Mustard Salmon

This bright and cheerful salmon dish flavored with lemon juice, brown sugar and mustard will surely be a wonderful addition to the dinner table. It's as tasty as it is beautiful.

Serving Size: 4

Preparation & Cooking Time: 25 minutes

Ingredients:

- Cooking spray
- 4 salmon fillets
- 2 tablespoons lemon juice
- 3 tablespoons mustard
- ¼ cup brown sugar

Instructions:

Spray your baking pan with oil.

Add the salmon to the baking pan.

Drizzle with the lemon juice.

Brush with the yellow mustard.

Top with the brown sugar.

Bake in the oven at 375 degrees F for 15 minutes or until flaky.

40. Lemon & Basil Salmon

No one will guess that this show-stopping meal is effortless to make!

Serving Size: 2

Preparation & Cooking Time: 20 minutes

Ingredients:

- 2 salmon fillets
- 1 tablespoon melted butter
- 1 tablespoon lemon juice
- 1 tablespoon fresh basil, minced
- Salt and pepper to taste
- Lemon wedges

Instructions:

Preheat your grill.

Place the salmon in a foil sheet.

In a bowl, mix the butter, lemon juice, basil, salt and pepper.

Brush the salmon with the mixture.

Fold the foil around the salmon.

Pinch the edges to seal.

Place the foil packets on top of the grill.

Grill for 15 minutes.

Open the foil packet carefully.

Garnish with the lemon wedges.

41. Ginger Mahi Mahi

Here's an Asian-inspired fish recipe that transforms mild mahi mahi into something unforgettable.

Serving Size: 4

Preparation & Cooking Time: 50 minutes

Ingredients:

- 3 tablespoons soy sauce
- 3 tablespoons balsamic vinegar
- 2 teaspoons olive oil
- 3 tablespoons honey
- 1 clove garlic, crushed
- 1 teaspoon ginger, grated
- 4 mahi mahi fillets
- Salt and pepper to taste
- 1 tablespoon vegetable oil

Instructions:

In a bowl, combine the soy sauce, vinegar, olive oil, honey, garlic and ginger.

Divide the mixture into two bowls.

Sprinkle both sides of the fish with the salt and pepper.

Add the fish to the first bowl. Reserve the second bowl.

Cover and refrigerate for 30 minutes.

Add the vegetable oil to a pan over medium high heat.

Cook the fish for 5 minutes per side or until flaky.

Transfer the fish to a serving plate.

Pour the reserved soy sauce mixture into the same pan.

Simmer for 10 minutes.

Pour the sauce over the fish and serve.

42. Ginger Honey Salmon

Looking for an alternative to the usual meat dishes you serve at home? Here's a winning recipe that everyone will surely enjoy—gingered honey salmon.

Serving Size: 6

Preparation & Cooking Time: 25 minutes

Ingredients:

- ¼ cup honey
- 1/3 cup soy sauce
- 1/3 cup orange juice
- 1 green onion, minced
- 1 teaspoon garlic powder
- 1 teaspoon ground ginger
- 1 ½ lb. salmon fillet

Instructions:

Mix the soy sauce, honey, orange juice, green onion, garlic powder and ground ginger in a bowl.

Add the salmon to a shallow dish.

Pour the mixture over the salmon.

Turn to coat.

Cover and refrigerate for 30 minutes.

Grill the salmon for 7 to 8 minutes per side.

43. Tuna Salad

Tuna flakes, mayo, sweet onion and celery blend nicely in this refreshing salad recipe that only takes 20 minutes to prepare.

Serving Size: 4

Preparation & Cooking Time: 20 minutes

Ingredients:

- 2/3 cup mayonnaise
- 12 oz. tuna flakes, drained
- ½ cup sweet onion, chopped
- 1 rib celery, chopped
- 1 teaspoon fresh parsley, minced
- Pepper to taste
- 4 tomatoes, sliced

Instructions:

Combine the mayo, tuna flakes, sweet onion, parsley and pepper in a bowl.

Mix well.

Serve with the tomato slices.

44. Tuna Steak & Pasta

If you're looking for something new and different to do with tuna, here's an idea that you'd be glad to have found—tuna steak served on top of pasta with tomato sauce.

Serving Size: 2

Preparation & Cooking Time: 30 minutes

Ingredients:

- 3 tablespoons olive oil, divided
- 8 tablespoons chicken broth, divided
- 1 teaspoon dried oregano, divided
- 1 teaspoon dried basil, divided
- Salt and pepper to taste
- 1 tuna steak, sliced in half
- ½ cup sweet onion, sliced thinly
- 1 cup canned diced tomatoes
- ¼ teaspoon brown sugar
- 3 oz. fettuccine (uncooked)

Instructions:

Mix 2 tablespoons olive oil, 2 tablespoons chicken broth, ¼ teaspoon dried oregano and ¼ teaspoon dried basil in a large bowl.

Add the tuna to the bowl.

Turn to coat.

Cover the bowl.

Refrigerate for 1 hour.

Add the remaining oil to a pan over medium heat.

Cook the onion for 5 minutes, stirring often.

Stir in the tomatoes and brown sugar.

Add the remaining wine and herbs.

Season with the salt and pepper.

Bring to a boil.

Reduce heat and simmer for 5 minutes.

Prepare the pasta according to the directions in the package.

Place the tuna in the tomato mixture, discarding the marinade.

Return to a boil.

Reduce heat and simmer for 6 minutes.

Toss the pasta in the tomato mixture.

Serve with the tuna steak on top.

45. Salmon with Walnuts & Ginger

Walnuts and ginger add flavor and texture to salmon in a way that will tantalize your taste buds.

Serving Size: 4

Preparation & Cooking Time: 30 minutes

Ingredients:

- 1 tablespoon soy sauce
- 1 tablespoon brown sugar
- 1 tablespoon Dijon mustard
- 1 teaspoon ground ginger
- Salt to taste
- 4 salmon fillets
- 1/3 cup walnuts, chopped
- Cooking spray

Instructions:

Preheat your oven to 425 degrees F.

In a bowl, mix the soy sauce, brown sugar, mustard, ground ginger and salt.

Brush both sides of the salmon with the mixture.

Top with the walnuts.

Transfer the fish to a baking pan sprayed with oil.

Bake in the oven for 15 minutes or until flaky.

46. Mahi Mahi & Veggies

For those who aren't too crazy about fish, this mahi mahi and vegetable recipe is a definite game-changer.

Serving Size: 4

Preparation & Cooking Time: 30 minutes

Ingredients:

- 3 tablespoons olive oil, divided
- 4 mahi mahi
- 1 sweet onion, sliced into rings
- ½ lb. baby Portobello mushrooms, sliced
- 3 sweet red peppers, sliced into strips
- 1/3 cup lemon juice
- Salt and pepper to taste
- 1/3 cup pine nuts
- ¼ cup fresh chives, minced

Instructions:

Pour 2 tablespoons olive oil into a pan over medium high heat.

Cook the fish fillets for 4 to 5 minutes per side.

Transfer to a plate.

Add the remaining olive oil.

Cook the onion, mushrooms and peppers for 5 minutes or until tender.

Drizzle with the lemon juice.

Season with the salt and pepper.

Top with the fish.

Top with the pine nuts and chives before serving.

47. Thai Salmon Rice Bowl

Here's a recipe that gives you a flavorful and satisfying meal without the fuss.

Serving Size: 4

Preparation & Cooking Time: 15 minutes

Ingredients:

- 4 salmon fillets
- ½ cup sesame ginger salad dressing, divided
- 3 cups cooked brown rice
- Salt to taste
- ½ cup fresh cilantro, chopped
- 1 cup carrot, sliced into strips
- Red cabbage, sliced

Instructions:

Preheat your oven to 400 degrees F.

Place the salmon in a baking pan.

Brush both sides with ¼ cup sesame ginger salad dressing.

Bake in the oven for 10 minutes or until flaky.

Toss the rice with the salt and cilantro.

Add the rice to serving bowls.

Top with the baked salmon, carrot and cabbage.

Serve with the remaining salad dressing.

48. Sage & Garlic Spiced Salmon

This speedy fish recipe can't be easier—simply flavor up salmon fillets with sage, garlic powder and pepper, and cook in the oven, and that's it! Serve this with green beans, fresh salad or rice.

Serving Size: 6

Preparation & Cooking Time: 20 minutes

Ingredients:

- 1 teaspoon garlic powder
- 2 tablespoons olive oil
- 2 tablespoons fresh sage, minced
- Salt and pepper to taste
- 6 salmon fillets

Instructions:

Preheat your oven to 375 degrees F.

In a bowl, combine the garlic powder, fresh sage, salt and pepper.

Season both sides of salmon with the garlic powder mixture.

Place the fish in a baking pan.

Bake in the oven for 10 to 15 minutes or until flaky.

49. Salmon with Lime & Cucumber Sauce

Lime juice, rice vinegar, cucumber and cilantro flavor up salmon in an incredible way that will surely make you say wow.

Serving Size: 10

Preparation & Cooking Time: 40 minutes

Ingredients:

- 2 tablespoons olive oil
- 2 tablespoons rice vinegar
- ¼ cup lime juice
- 1 tablespoon lime zest
- 4 teaspoons sugar
- ½ teaspoon ground coriander
- 1/3 cup fresh cilantro, chopped
- 1 tablespoon onion, chopped
- 2 teaspoons ginger, minced
- 2 cloves garlic, minced
- 2 cucumbers, chopped
- Salt and pepper to taste

Salmon

- 1 tablespoon olive oil
- 1/3 cup ginger, minced
- 1 tablespoon lime juice
- Salt and pepper to taste
- 10 salmon fillets

Instructions:

Combine the olive oil, rice vinegar, lime juice, lime zest, sugar, ground coriander, fresh cilantro, onion, ginger, garlic, cucumbers, salt and pepper in a blender or food processor.

Process until pureed.

In a bowl, mix the olive oil, ginger, lime juice, salt and pepper.

Brush the salmon with the mixture.

Grill the fish over medium high heat for 5 to 6 minutes per side or until flaky.

Serve the fish with the sauce.

50. Salmon with Horseradish

Flavor up salmon with a combination of horseradish, sour cream and pistachios for a crunchy and delectable fish dish that you and your family will find enticing.

Serving Size: 6

Preparation & Cooking Time: 30 minutes

Ingredients:

- 6 salmon fillets (4 ounces each)
- 1/3 cup sour cream
- 2/3 cup breadcrumbs
- 2/3 cup pistachios, chopped
- ½ cup shallots, minced
- 2 tablespoons olive oil
- 2 tablespoons horseradish
- 1 tablespoon fresh dill, minced
- ½ teaspoon lemon zest
- ¼ teaspoon red pepper flakes, crushed
- 1 clove garlic, minced

Instructions:

Preheat your oven to 350 degrees F.

Add the salmon to a baking pan.

Spread the sour cream on top of the fish fillet.

In a bowl, mix the remaining ingredients.

Press the mixture on top of the salmon fillets.

Bake in the oven for 15 minutes or until flaky.

Conclusion

You've reached the end of the recipe collection and for sure, you can't wait to try all of these.

With these options, you won't run out of ideas to rotate each week.

And because these are truly delicious, you probably won't just eat two servings per week, but even more.

Enjoy!

Biography

Cooking is second nature to Olivia. This is not a surprise as she comes from a family of chefs. Cooking runs in the Rana family, and it is no wonder that Olivia didn't bother trying to find her root in life.

It was as if her path in life had been preordained for her. She knew that all she wanted to do in life was to be a food expert.

So, after college, she started a small restaurant in her town and launched a culinary school by the side.

Both businesses are doing well, and Olivia has expanded the businesses to a very admirable length.

Afterword

Readers like you are the reason I get up in the morning. I am delighted that you decided to download and read my Books.

I can't thank you enough for choosing healthy living via your choice to engage in healthy and creative cooking. It means a lot to me because I poured my heart and passion into every page of this cookbook. And this is why I hope that you'd get absolute fulfillment from reading and exploring cooking with this recipe book.

I know that there are lots of similar culinary content like this everywhere, but it gives me joy that you chose mine. Hence, I'd appreciate it if you could help with your thoughts about this book. Feedback from customers helps me do better, so I don't mind getting a few from you.

You can do that by leaving a review on Amazon.com.

Thanks!

Olivia Rana

Printed in Great Britain
by Amazon